Butterfly Squad is a revolutionary new worldwide healthcare brand for children.

We develop ground-breaking, cutting edge, digital and real world platforms that have a singular goal... to drive down the devastating statistics that are effecting our children.

Our purpose is to change the world by ensuring that there is **no kid left behind** when it comes to their mental and physical health.

Sign up to watch our free cartoons that teach children how to recognise and process their emotions at **butterflysquad.rocks/no-kid-left-behind**

The creation of powerful, future generations starts with Butterfly Squad!

Scan this QR code on your smartphone to watch **16 FREE CARTOONS** that show you how to be strong and powerful!

Hello :)

I'm Nik. Welcome to Butterfly Squad.

We show kids (just like you) how to be the BEST version of themselves, whatever that may look like!

We will train you how to be a powerful ninja of your own mind! We will make you VERY powerful! It's a bit like magic. Each book reveals a new super power to put YOU in charge of your own life.

But remember, these books can only show you how, they can't do it for you... only YOU have the power to do that!

YOU HAVE THE POWER TO MAKE YOUR OWN CHANGES!

Are you ready? Then turn the page and let's go!

Nik x

'WHERE THE MAGIC HAPPENS'
CHILDRENS BOOKS
First published in Great Britain
in 2024 by Where The Magic
Happens.

ISBN: 978-1-3999-8781-3

Produced for Squad Fit LTD by
Copper Brown.
www.copperbrown.co.uk

Printed and bound by Amazon
all around the world.

#NoKidLeftBehind
www.butterflysquad.rocks/No-Kid-Left-Behind
@ButterflySquadRocks

For Destiny & Hope,
my beautiful daughters and
the light of my life. Without
you, Butterfly Squad would
not exist.

And to all the children of the
world, you are all special in
your own unique way...
every single one of you!

Nicole Antoniou

Parrot? Fairy? CHOOSE!

Written by
Nicole Antoniou
& Luke Cutler

Illustrated by
Alina Klymchuk

Minny was playing in the playground, her most favourite place of all.

All of a sudden, Minny went flying.

SPLOoooooOOOOSH

She looks up to see Mark, a boy from her class who is always doing mean things.

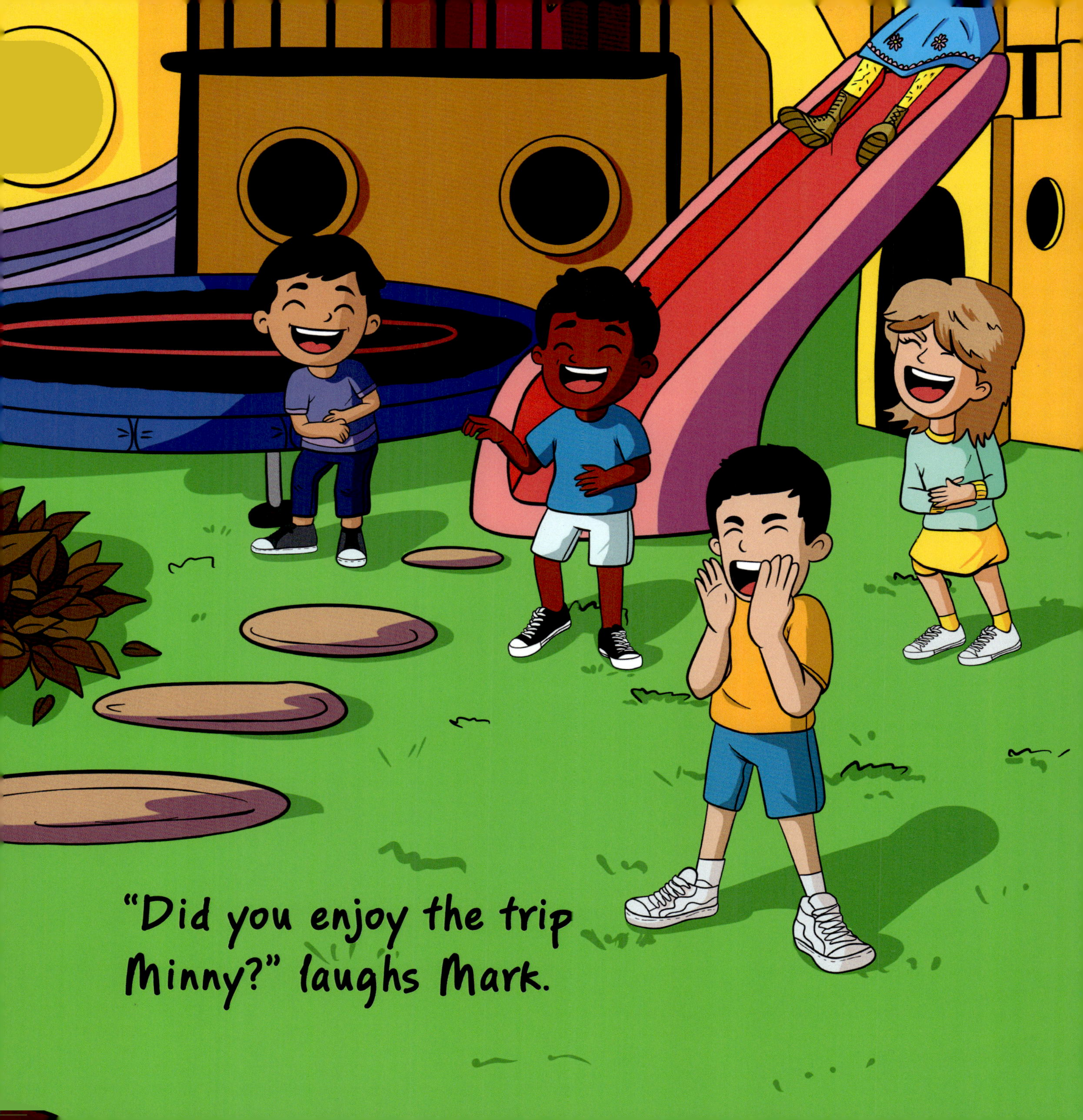

"Did you enjoy the trip Minny?" laughs Mark.

Minny heard that little voice, you know the one... the bad one that always tries to get you in trouble.

She started to get really angry...

Minny could feel her blood begin to boil until suddenly...
SHE EXPLODED!

"GET HIM MINNY!?!"
ordered her parrot.

Then she heard that other voice. You know the one! The kind one that always looks out for you, no matter what!

Minny chose not to listen to her parrot! Instead she chose to spend her time having fun with her friends.

While Minny and her friends played... her parrot got a little smaller. It was so slight she didn't even notice.

And when parrots get smaller... fairies get BIGGER.

After playtime was 'arts and crafts'.
Minny loved being creative.

All of a sudden, Minny's tower came crashing down.
GLUE
There was that voice again. It was a little quieter this time but she could still hear it!

"Get him back Minny..." insisted her parrot.

"It would be sooooooooooooooooooo EASY!"

It WOULD have been easy, and Minny really did want to get him back...

But her fairy was a little bigger, and a little louder which made her a little easier to listen to. Minny picked everything up, dusted it off and chose to start again.

Somehow her creation turned out even better than before...

The more Minny chose to listen to her fairy, the more POWERFUL it became.

And her parrot became even smaller!

Minny LOVED lunch time.
She got to try colourful
new food while hanging out
with her friends.

But something wasn't quite right...
Mark had put chilli powder in her food!!

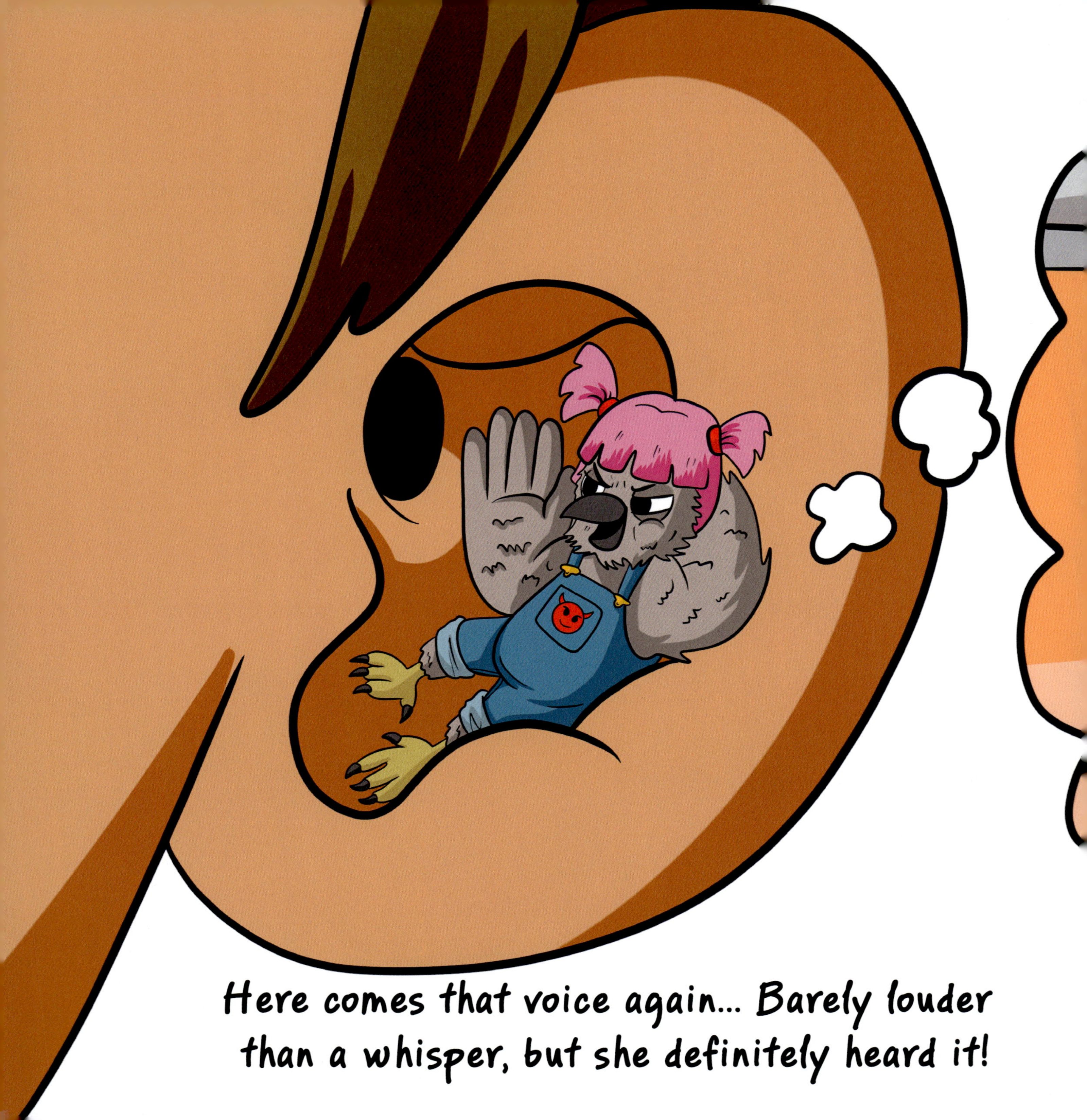

Here comes that voice again... Barely louder than a whisper, but she definitely heard it!

But her fairy was much bigger and much louder, so it was much easier to ignore her parrot.

Minny was even given a mega ice cream to cool down her tongue and she chose to share it with everyone.

After a while, Minny could barely hear her parrot. It never left her, but it was so small that it was really easy to ignore. Minny and her fairy were best friends for life.

And as for Mark, well...

BE CAREFUL WHO YOU LISTEN TO!

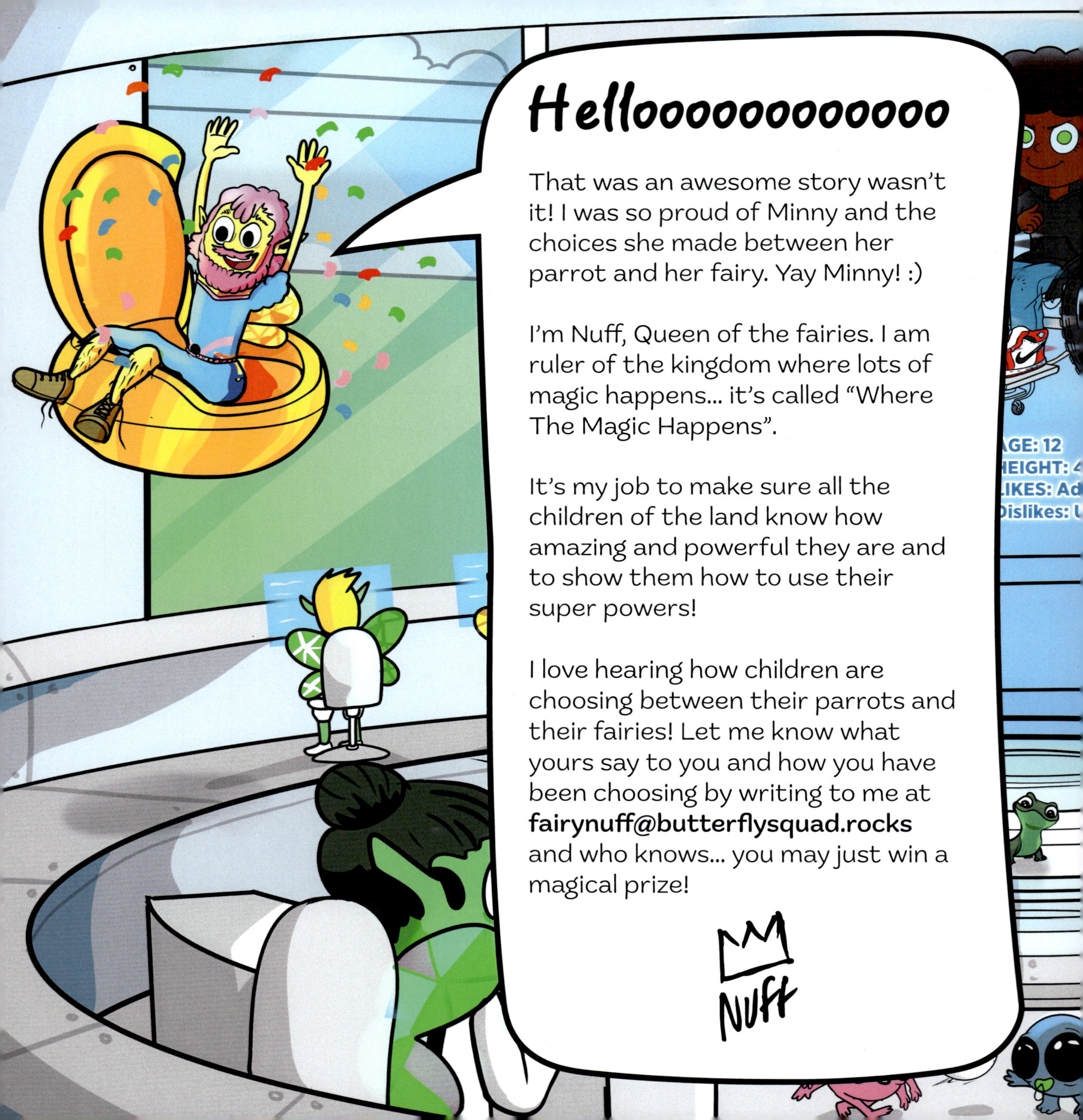
Hellooooooooooooo
That was an awesome story wasn't it! I was so proud of Minny and the choices she made between her parrot and her fairy. Yay Minny! :)
I'm Nuff, Queen of the fairies. I am ruler of the kingdom where lots of magic happens... it's called "Where The Magic Happens".
It's my job to make sure all the children of the land know how amazing and powerful they are and to show them how to use their super powers!
I love hearing how children are choosing between their parrots and their fairies! Let me know what yours say to you and how you have been choosing by writing to me at **fairynuff@butterflysquad.rocks** and who knows... you may just win a magical prize!
NUFF

DID YOU SEE ME??

If you look back through the book, you will notice that I am always around somewhere.

Have fun trying to find me and if you get stuck, turn this book upside down and check out the answers at the bottom of the page... or is it now the top of the page?

OH! And don't forget that you can watch my awesome cartoons that teach you all about being a powerful ninja of your own mind: www.butterflysquad.rocks/no-kid-left-behind

TURN THE BOOK UPSIDE DOWN!!!!